MW00511489

Great Big Praise

for a Great BIG God

117 Fun, Exciting, Singable Songs
for Younger Kids

Compiled by Tom Fettke and Ken Bible

Edited by Tom Fettke

lillenas PUBLISHING COMPANY

KANSAS CITY, MO 64141

www.lillenas.com

CHILDREN AND MUSIC are a natural combination. That's why we're happy to present GREAT BIG PRAISE, an indispensable resource for children in Sunday school, children's choir, children's church, VBS, camps, Christian schools, and home. Many terrific songs, on a wide variety of topics, are included in either of two volumes – Book 1 is for younger children (preschool - 2nd grade), and Book 2 is for older children (3rd - 6th grade). Songs in both books work for children of all ages.

The variety of companion products accompanying this book helps make presentation of these songs easy and memorable with long-lasting effect. Split-channel trax, stereo recordings, and even some fun activities for several of the songs in the book combine to offer a package no children's program should be without.

Great Big Praise is the official music for WordAction's *Faith Connections* curriculum, but it is designed to work equally well with any curriculum.

The selection of the songs in GREAT BIG PRAISE was the work of two committees:

Executive Committee:	**Advisory Committee:**
George Baldwin	Harold Burgmayer
Lynda Boardman	Tom Felder
Dorothy Hitzka	Virginia Folsom
John Mathias	Sheryl Graeflin
Blaine Smith	Melissa Hammer
Mark York	William Himes
	Marva Hoopes
	Deanna Patrick
	Carolyn Pickering
	Becki Privett
	George Pryor
	Deletta Tompkins

Contents

Praising God   songs   1 – 20

God's Creation   songs   21 – 30

God's Love and Care   songs   31 – 39

Bible Songs and Stories   songs   40 – 59

God Saves Us   songs   60 – 66

Serving God and Others   songs   67 – 78

Talking with God   songs   79 – 82

God's Church   songs   83 – 86

Special Times and Seasons   songs   87 – 101

    Christmas   songs   87 – 92

    Easter   songs   93 – 96

    Patriotic   song   97

    Thanksgiving   songs   98 – 101

Activity and Self Concept   songs 102 – 117

1 He Is the King of Kings

Words and Music by
VIRGIL MEARES

Children may clap their hands or use rhythm instruments where indicated in the song.

King. His name is Je-sus, Je-sus, Je-sus, Je-sus;

O_____ He is the King.

Jesus, I Love You

2

Words and Music by
OTIS SKILLINGS

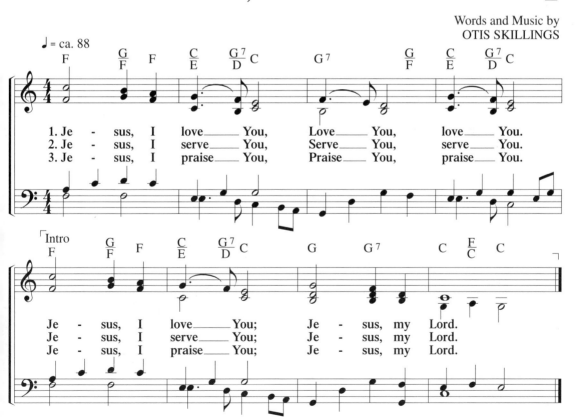

1. Je - sus, I love____ You, Love____ You, love____ You.
2. Je - sus, I serve____ You, Serve____ You, serve____ You.
3. Je - sus, I praise____ You, Praise____ You, praise____ You.

Je - sus, I love____ You; Je - sus, my Lord.
Je - sus, I serve____ You; Je - sus, my Lord.
Je - sus, I praise____ You; Je - sus, my Lord.

v. 1 -- Children cross their arms over their chests to illustrate "love".
v. 2 -- Children open their arms out, palms up, to illustrate "serve".
v. 3 -- Children raise their arms to heaven to illustrate "praise".

3

This Is the Day

Words and Music by
LES GARRETT

1. Leader sings.   2. Children sing.   3. All sing.

Alleluia

4

Words and Music by
JERRY SINCLAIR

This is the day, this is the day that the Lord has made.

1. Al - le - lu - ia, Al - le - lu - ia, Al - le - lu - ia, Al - le - lu - ia, Al - le - lu - ia, Al - le - lu - ia!
2. He's my Sav - ior, He's my Sav - ior, He's my Sav - ior, He's my Sav - ior, He's my Sav - ior, He's my Sav - ior!
3. I will praise Him, I will praise Him, I will praise Him, I will praise Him, I will praise Him, I will praise Him!

5 Make a Joyful Noise unto the Lord

Words and Music by
JIMMY and CAROL OWENS

*May be sung as a 3-part round.

Children may tap or clap their hands where indicated by X.
Children may use their voices or rhythm instruments where indicated by 0.

Ho Ho Hosanna

Traditional
Arranged by David McDonald

Ho - ho - ho - ho - san - na! Ha - ha - ha - le -

lu - jah! He He He He saved me,

I've got the joy of the Lord! Lord!

I've got the joy of the Lord! I've got the joy of the Lord!

Explain to the children that the words "Hosanna" and "Hallelujah" are words used in Bible times to thank God. Ask them to say other words they can use to thank Him.

7 He Has Made Me Glad

Words and Music by
LEONA VON BRETHORST

I will en - ter His gates with thanks - giv - ing in my heart; I will en - ter His courts with

Praising God

He has made me glad.

8   O How I Love Jesus

Unknown

O how I love Je - sus. O
how I love Je - sus. O how I love
Je - sus, Be - cause He first loved me.

Ask the children to tell ways that we show Jesus we love Him. Ask the children to tell ways that Jesus shows His love for us.

I Like to Sing About Jesus

Words and Music by
NAN GRANTHAM

Hallelujah!

Traditional

Divide the children into two groups; for example, boys and girls. Group I stands on "Hallelu" but sits on "Praise ye the Lord."
Group 2 sits on "Hallelu" but stands on "Praise ye the Lord". Have fun and get some exercise with this song.

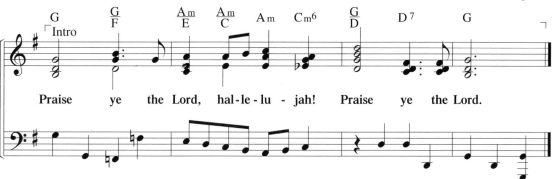

Praise ye the Lord, hal-le-lu - jah! Praise ye the Lord.

I Will Sing Songs of Joy

11

Words adapted from Psalm.

CRYSTAL DAVIS CLAY

I will sing songs of joy to the Lord. For

great is the Lord, and great-ly to be praised!

1. Praise Him with my heart,
2. Praise Him with my life,
3. Praise Him with my voice,

Praise Him with my heart,
Praise Him with my life,   I will   sing songs of joy   to the Lord.
Praise Him with my voice,

12

Stand Up and Clap

Words and Music by
CHERRY TADLOCK

Children clap as indicated by X.

Praising God

Down In My Heart

Words and Music by
GEORGE W. COOKE
Arranged by Tom Fettke

1. I have the joy, joy, joy, joy down in my heart, Down in my heart, down in my heart. I have the joy, joy, joy, joy down in my heart; Down in my heart to stay.

2. I have the peace that pass-eth un-der-stand-ing down in my heart, Down in my heart, down in my heart. I have the peace that pass-eth un-der-stand-ing down in my heart; Down in my heart to stay.

3. I have the love of Je-sus, love of Je-sus down in my heart, Down in my heart, down in my heart. I have the love of Je-sus, love of Je-sus down in my heart; Down in my heart to stay.

2. I have the
3. I have the

14 My God Is So Big

Unknown

1. Stand with hands on hips.   2. Make big muscles out to the side.   3. Point up to the heavens.   4. Make "waves" with hands.
5. Make elephant trunk with arm.

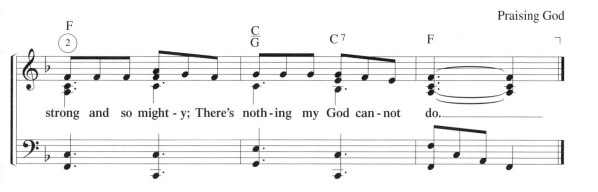

strong and so might - y; There's noth-ing my God can-not do.

With My Voice

15

Words and Music by
JOYCE GRIFFITTS

1. With my voice I can talk to Je - sus; With my
2. With my voice I can talk and ① whis - per; With my

voice I can sing His name; With my voice I can
voice I can ② shout and sing; With my voice I can

① whis - per soft - ly; He hears just the same.
wor - ship Je - sus, And my prais - es bring.

1. Children whisper softly.   2. Children sing loudly.

16 Sing Hallelujah!

Words and Music by
PATRICIA LOU HARRIS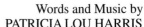

v. 2, hands clap on each beat.

* "Allelu," Music traditional.

Praising God

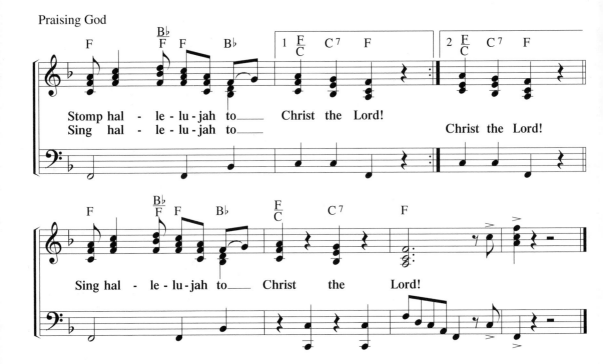

17   Clap, Clap, Clap

GRACE ABBOTT

Traditional

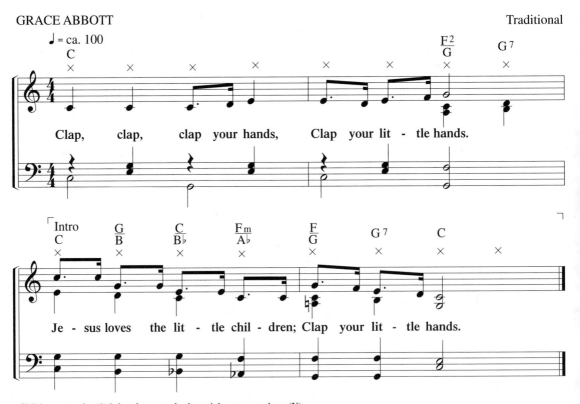

Children may clap their hands or tap rhythm sticks on every beat (X).

Praise Him, Praise Him

Unknown
Arranged by Tom Fettke

19 Praise the Lord, All Creation

LINDA REBUCK

DAVID HUNTSINGER
and BONNIE HUNTSINGER

♩ = ca. 138

1. Praise the Lord, all cre-a-tion;
2. All the stars in the heav-ens;
3. Wor-ship Him, all cre-a-tion;

(clap, clap)* Praise the Lord.
(clap, clap) Praise the Lord.
(clap, clap) Praise the Lord.

Praise the Lord,
All the stars
Wor-ship Him,

all cre-a-tion; (clap, clap) Praise the Lord.
in the heav-ens; (clap, clap) Praise the Lord.
all cre-a-tion; (clap, clap) Praise the Lord.

*Rhythm instruments may be used in addition to claps.

20 Rejoice in the Lord Always

Adapted from Philippians 4:4 — Traditional

* May be sung as a 4-part round. Accompaniment is optional.

He's Got the Whole World
in His Hands

Spiritual
Arranged by Lyndell Leatherman

22 God Made Me

MARGARET W. SELF

JEANNE P. LAWLER

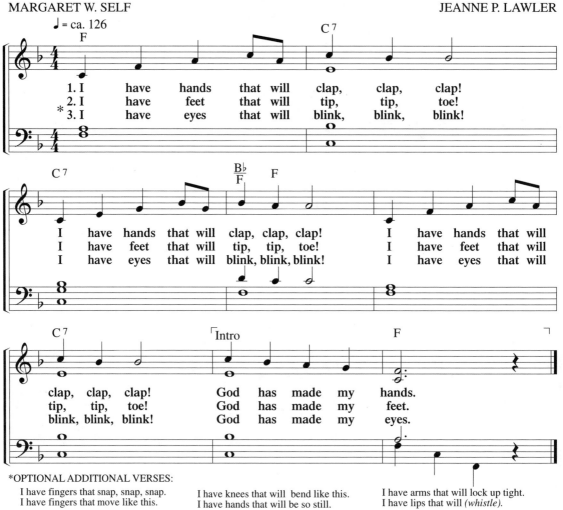

♩ = ca. 126

1. I have hands that will clap, clap, clap!
2. I have feet that will tip, tip, toe!
*3. I have eyes that will blink, blink, blink!

I have hands that will clap, clap, clap! I have hands that will
I have feet that will tip, tip, toe! I have feet that will
I have eyes that will blink, blink, blink! I have eyes that will

clap, clap, clap! God has made my hands.
tip, tip, toe! God has made my feet.
blink, blink, blink! God has made my eyes.

*OPTIONAL ADDITIONAL VERSES:

I have fingers that snap, snap, snap.   I have knees that will bend like this.   I have arms that will lock up tight.
I have fingers that move like this.   I have hands that will be so still.   I have lips that will *(whistle).*

Children should do appropriate motions with each verse.

23 God Made the Animals

LYNETTE DUPLAIN

Traditional

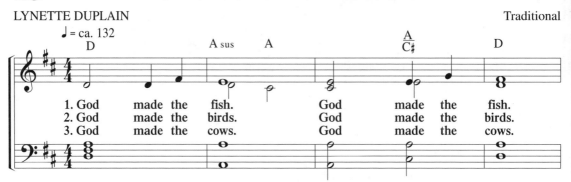

♩ = ca. 132

1. God made the fish. God made the fish.
2. God made the birds. God made the birds.
3. God made the cows. God made the cows.

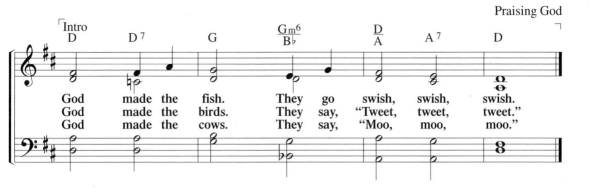

God made the fish. They go swish, swish, swish.
God made the birds. They say, "Tweet, tweet, tweet."
God made the cows. They say, "Moo, moo, moo."

I'm So Glad

24

ETHEL M. GREENAWALT

Traditional
Arranged by Lyndell Leatherman

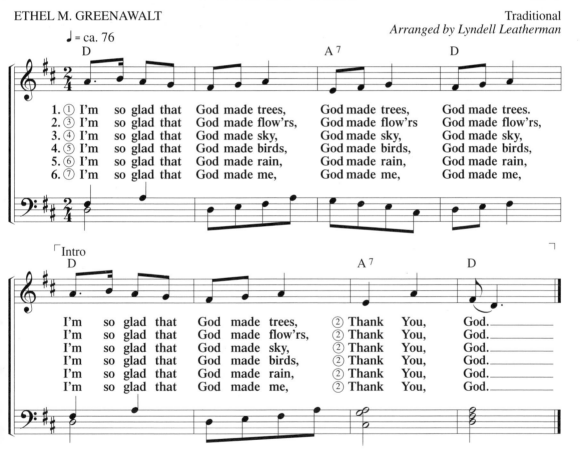

1. ① I'm so glad that God made trees, God made trees, God made trees.
2. ③ I'm so glad that God made flow'rs, God made flow'rs, God made flow'rs,
3. ④ I'm so glad that God made sky, God made sky, God made sky,
4. ⑤ I'm so glad that God made birds, God made birds, God made birds,
5. ⑥ I'm so glad that God made rain, God made rain, God made rain,
6. ⑦ I'm so glad that God made me, God made me, God made me,

I'm so glad that God made trees, ② Thank You, God.
I'm so glad that God made flow'rs, ② Thank You, God.
I'm so glad that God made sky, ② Thank You, God.
I'm so glad that God made birds, ② Thank You, God.
I'm so glad that God made rain, ② Thank You, God.
I'm so glad that God made me, ② Thank You, God.

Motions:
1. Children stand tall with arms stretched upward and swaying like tree branches.
2. Fold hands and bow heads.
3. Kneel and pretend to be picking flowers.
4. Point to sky.
5. Move arms to imitate birds' wings.
6. Wiggle fingers while lowering arms to imitate falling raindrops.
7. Children point to themselves.

Verses 1,3,4 and 6 on recording.

25

I Often Think of God

Words and Music by
CARL PERRY

1. When I see a star twink-ling in the night, I
of-ten think of God. When I see the moon so____

2. When I hear a bird be-gin to sing, I
of-ten think of God. When I see a bee with its

big and bright, I of-ten think of God.
ti-ny wings, I of-ten think of God.

Option: Teacher sing first phrase, children sing "I often think of God."

26

That's Good

Words and Music by
DENNIS and NAN ALLEN

God's Creation

God's Creation

27 God Saw All

MELISSA K. HAMMER

Traditional
Arranged by David McDonald

 = ca. 84

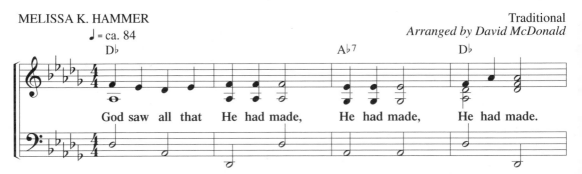

God saw all that He had made, He had made, He had made.

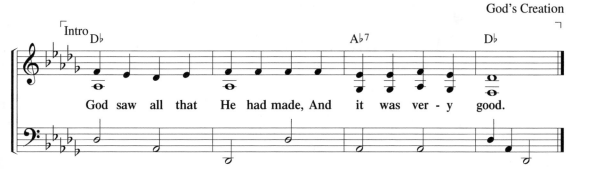

Who Made You?

28

Words and Music by
JULIE BARRIER

*Grace notes may be omitted for a beginning pianist.

While teacher sings, children can pretend to be each of the animals and other things that God made. Children join singing on "God made you!"

29 All Creatures Great and Small

Words and Music by
CATHY SPURR, DAVID SPURR
and DEBBY MCNEIL

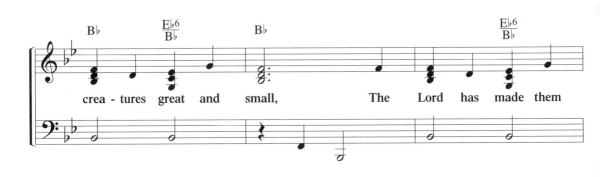

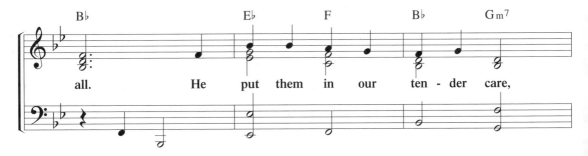

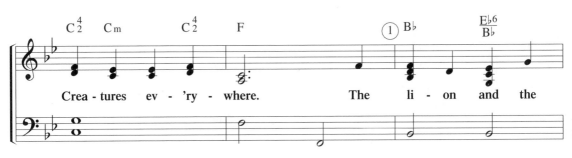

1. Children stand up tall. 2. Children make themselves small. 3. Make "horns" on their heads. 4. Pretend to swim. Pretend to fly.
6. Hop 7. Pretend to push away brush as if in a dense jungle. 8. Pretend to climb. 9. Pretend to stroke "whiskers". 10. Make "ears."

God's Creation

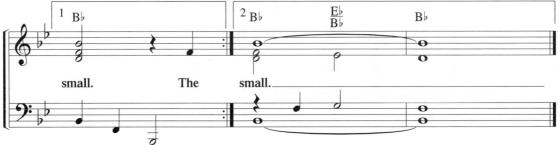

Everything Was Made by God

30

Words and Music by
TINA ENGLISH

Sing the song through several times, stopping between to ask the chldren to name something they see that God made.

31 Jesus Loves the Little Children

C.H. WOOLSTON

GEORGE F. ROOT

1. Je - sus loves the lit - tle chil - dren, All the chil-dren of the
2. Je - sus died for all the chil - dren, All the chil-dren of the

world. Red and yel - low, black and white, They are pre-cious in His sight—
world. Red and yel - low, black and white, They are pre-cious in His sight—

Intro

Je - sus loves the lit - tle chil - dren of the world.
Je - sus died for all the chil - dren of the world.

32 God Is Love

MELISSA K. HAMMER

Traditional
Arranged by David McDonald

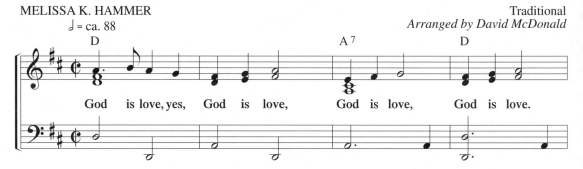

God is love, yes, God is love, God is love, God is love.

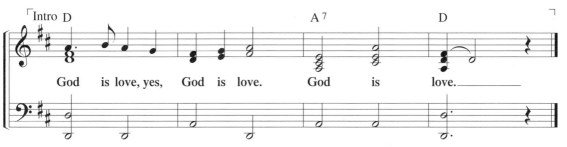

Jesus Loves Me, Me, Me

33

Words and Music by
PENNIE AUST

34 God Is Always There

Words and Music by
KATHIE HILL

He nev-er sleeps, He nev-er slum-bers while I'm un-der His care. When I close my eyes I re-al-ize that God is

35 Jesus Loves Me

ANNA B. WARNER

WILLIAM B. BRADBURY

1. Je - sus loves me this I know, For the Bi - ble tells me so.
2. Je - sus loves me! He who died Heav-en's gates to o - pen wide.

Lit - tle ones to Him be - long; They are weak, but He is strong.
He will wash a - way my sin, Let His lit - tle child come in.

Yes, Je - sus loves me. Yes, Je - sus loves me.

Yes, Je - sus loves me, The Bi - ble tells me so.

All Night, All Day

36

KEN BIBLE and Traditional

Spiritual
Arranged by Lyndell Leatherman

1. The sun is set-ting in the west; An-gels watch-in' o-ver me, my Lord. I
2. Your love stays with me thro' the night; An-gels watch-in' o-ver me, my Lord. You
3. I rise to start a brand new day; An-gels watch-in' o-ver me, my Lord. And

close my eyes and gent-ly rest; An-gels watch-in' o-ver me.
wake me with the morn-ing light; An-gels watch-in' o-ver me.
all the while I work or pray; An-gels watch-in' o-ver me.

All night, all day, An-gels watch-in' o-ver me, my Lord.

Intro

All night, all day, An-gels watch-in' o-ver me.

37 God Is Bigger

Words and Music by
PHIL VISCHER

God is big-ger than the bo-gey-man. He's big-ger than God-zil-la, or the mon-sters on T. V. O

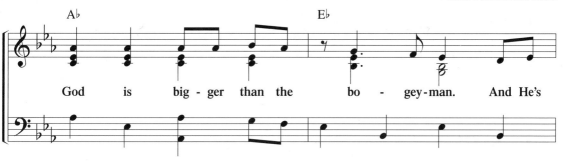

God is big-ger than the bo - gey-man. And He's

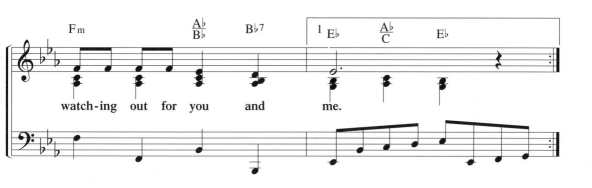

watch-ing out for you and me.

me. And He's watch-ing out for you and

me. And He's watch-ing out for you and me.

38 God Cares for You and Me

Traditional
Arranged by David McDonald

cares for you and me;_____ God cares for you and
cares for you and me;_____ God cares for you and
cares for you and me;_____ God cares for you and

me;_____ *He gives us home and food and clothes; God
me;_____ He lights the sky with stars at night; God
me;_____ I learn at Sun - day School and church; God

cares for you and me._____ 2. God
cares for you and me._____ 3. God
cares for you and me.

*For this line, substitute these words when appropriate:
He sends His shining angels bright.
He gives us aunts and uncles dear.
(or make up your own.)

Enough Love

LINDA REBUCK

TOM FETTKE

40 I Wonder How It Felt

WILLIAM J. GAITHER
and GLORIA GAITHER

WILLIAM J. GAITHER

*1. I won-der how it felt to wake up in the bel-ly of a whale.
(2.) I won-der how it felt to meet big Go-li-ath in the field.
(3.) I won-der how it'd be to watch your ba-by broth-er in the Nile;
(4.) I won-der how it felt to spend the night with No-ah in the zoo;

I won-der how it felt to spend the night with Si-las in the jail.
I won-der how it felt to know the mouths of li-ons have been sealed.
I won-der who would come, a prin-cess or a hun-gry croc-o-dile.
I won-der how it felt to sleep be-side a smell-y kan-ga-roo.

*Recording has verses 1, 3 and 4.

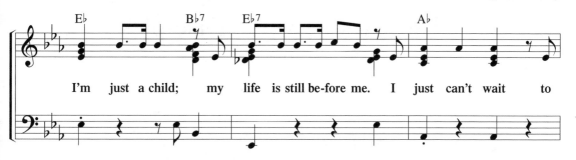

I'm just a child; my life is still be-fore me. I just can't wait to

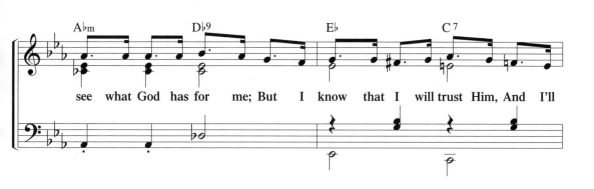

see what God has for me; But I know that I will trust Him, And I'll

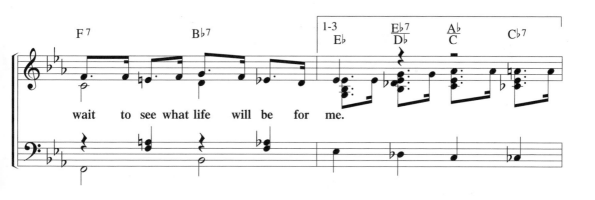

wait to see what life will be for me.

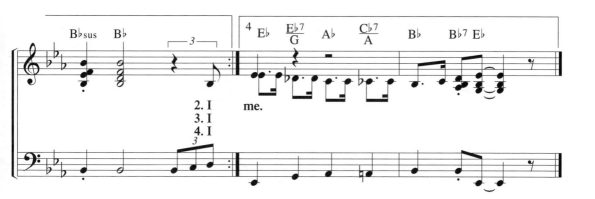

2. I
3. I
4. I

me.

41 There Were Twelve Disciples

Unknown

GEORGE A. MINOR

We are His dis-ci-ples; I am one, are you? We His work must do.

Psalm 119:11

42

Pslam 119:11

DWIGHT UPHAUS

I have hid-den Your Word in my heart That I might not sin, O Lord. I have hid-den Your Word in my heart That I might not sin a-gainst You, That I might not sin a-gainst You.

43 Arky, Arky

Traditional

1. The Lord____ told No-ah, "There's gon-na be a ①flood-y, flood-y."
2. The Lord____ told No-ah to build_him an ⑤ark-y, ark-y.
3. The an-i-mals, the an-i-mals– they came_in by ⑦two-sies, two-sies.
4. It rained____ and poured____ for ⅞ for-ty ⑨day-sies, day-sies.
5. The sun____ came out____ and dried_up the ⑪land-y, land-y.

Lord____ told No-ah, "There's gon-na be a flood-y, flood-y."
Lord____ told No-ah to build_him an ark-y, ark-y.
An-i-mals, the an-i-mals– they came_in by two-sies, two-sies.
Rained____ and poured____ for ⅞ for-ty day-sies, day-sies.
Sun____ came out____ and dried_up the land-y, land-y.

② Get these an-i-mals out of the mud-dy, mud-dy,
⑥ Build it out____ of go-pher bark-y, bark-y,
⑧ El-e-phants____ and kan-ga-roo-sies, roo-sies,
⑩ Al-most drove____ those an-i-mals cra-zy, cra-zy,
⑫ Ev-'ry-thing____ was fine____ and dand-y, dand-y,

1. Wiggle fingers up to down for rain.
2. Point "out" with thumb.
3. Stand up.
4. Sit.
5. Pretend to hammer a nail.
6. Pretend to climb a tree.
7. Make "two" fingers.
8. Act like an elephant or hop like a kangaroo.
9. Show "ten" fingers four times.
10. Circle ear with finger like "crazy."
11. Make sunburst around face with hands.
12. Make "okay" sign with fingers.

44 Every Word of the Lord Is True

Words and Music by
JANET MCMAHAN-WILSON

Ev - 'ry

word of the Lord___ is true, Ev-'ry word of the Lord___ is

true. God wrote them in the Bi - ble for me and you, Ev-'ry

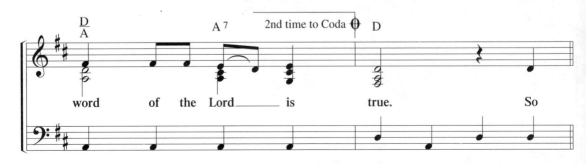

word of the Lord_____ is true. So

keep His words deep in your heart, They'll

be with you where-ev-er you are. Ev-'ry

CODA

true. Ev-'ry word of the Lord is true.

I Open My Bible and Read 45

Words and Music by
PHEROBA THOMAS

I o-pen my Bi-ble and read; *"God loves me." _____

*Substitute: "Je-sus lives"; "Be ye kind"; "God made me"; etc.
Option: For stronger reinforcement of ideas, sing each verse twice.

46

When I Am Afraid

Adapted from Psalm 56:3-4
by FRANK HERNANDEZ

FRANK HERNANDEZ
arranged by Emily Brink

47 The B-I-B-L-E

DWIGHT UPHAUS

Traditional

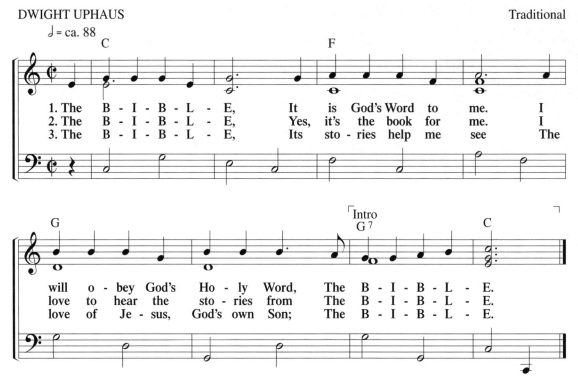

1. The B-I-B-L-E, It is God's Word to me. I
2. The B-I-B-L-E, Yes, it's the book for me. I
3. The B-I-B-L-E, Its sto-ries help me see The

1. will o-bey God's Ho-ly Word, The B-I-B-L-E.
2. love to hear the sto-ries from The B-I-B-L-E.
3. love of Je-sus, God's own Son; The B-I-B-L-E.

48 Jesus Grew and Grew

Words and Music by
BARBARA EBERT
Arranged by Lyndell Leatherman

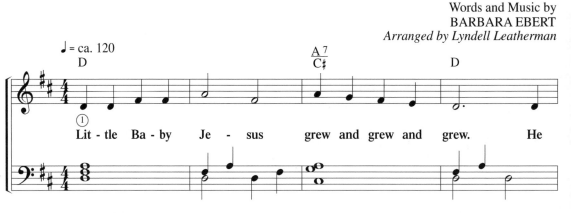

Lit-tle Ba-by Je-sus grew and grew and grew. He

1. Pretend to rock a baby.
2. Walk in place.
3. Make "talk" hands.
4. Fold hands in prayer.

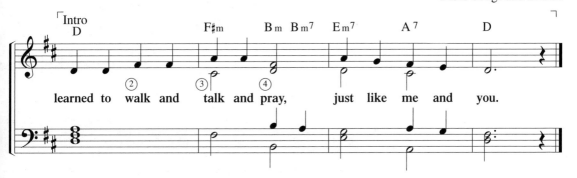

learned to walk and talk and pray, just like me and you.

I Will Listen

49

LOIS L. CURLY

Adapted from Vincent Novello
Arranged by Lyndell Leatherman

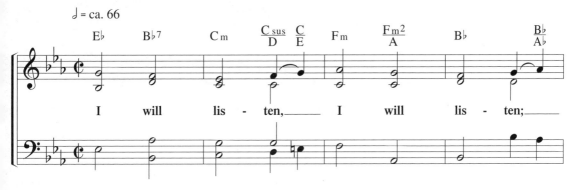

I will lis - ten,____ I will lis - ten;____

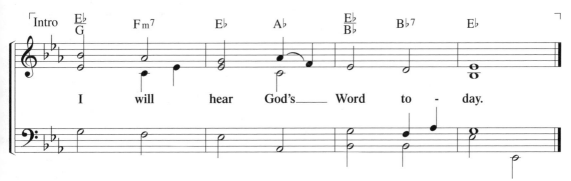

I will hear God's____ Word to - day.

Read the following scriptures to the children. Have them memorize the passages:
Psalm 85:8 — "I will listen to what God the LORD will say."
Psalm 119:11 — "I have hidden Your Word in my heart that I might not sin against You."

Ask the children what God's Word says about love, doing right, obeying parents, etc.

50 How Did Moses Cross the Red Sea?

Words and Music by
HUGH MITCHELL

♩ = ca. 120

How did Mo-ses cross the Red Sea? How did Mo-ses cross the

Red Sea? How did Mo-ses cross the Red Sea? How

did He get a - cross? Did he swim? No, no. Did he

51   The Wise Man and the Foolish Man

Adapted from Matthew 7:24-27

Unknown

1. Pound one fist in the palm of the other hand.
2. Wiggle fingers up to down making "rain."
3. Pound fist in palm hard.
4. Pound open palm in the palm of the other hand.
5. Pound open palm hard in the palm of the other hand.

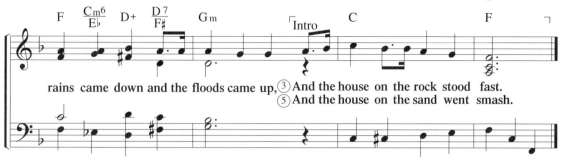

rains came down and the floods came up, ③ And the house on the rock stood fast.
⑤ And the house on the sand went smash.

Love One Another

52

Adapted from John 15:12

EVELYN BEALS

"Love one an-oth - er,
Love one an-oth - er." Je - sus said, Je - sus said. "Love one an-oth - er,
Love one an-oth - er." Je - sus said, "Love one an-oth - er."

53 This Is My Commandment

Adapted from John 15:12

Anonymous

♩ = ca. 120

This is my com-mand-ment that you love one an-oth - er, that your

joy may be full. full. That your joy may be

full, that your joy may be full. This is my com-mand-ment that you

love one an-oth - er, that your joy may be full.

Zaccheus

Traditional

Motions:
1. Hands in front, right palm raised above left palm.
2. Move palms closer together
3. Alternate hands in climbing motion.

4. Shade eyes with right hand and look down.
5. Shade eyes with right hand and look up.
6. Look up, gesture to Zaccheus to come down.
7. Clap hands on accented beats.

55 Abraham

JEFF SMITH
♩ = ca. 168

Traditional
Arranged by Tom Fettke

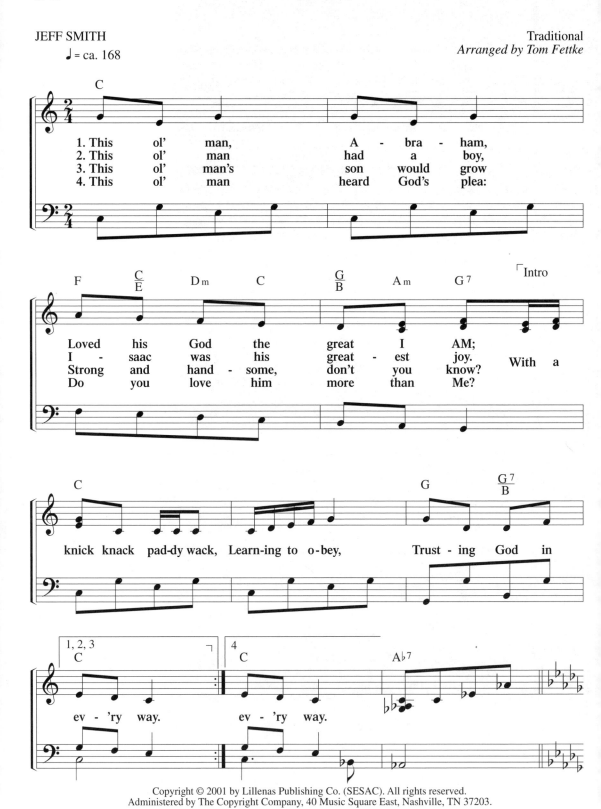

1. This ol' man, Abraham, Loved his God the great I AM;
2. This ol' man had a boy, Isaac was his greatest joy. With a
3. This ol' man's son would grow Strong and handsome, don't you know?
4. This ol' man heard God's plea: Do you love him more than Me?

knick knack pad-dy wack, Learn-ing to o-bey, Trust-ing God in

1, 2, 3
ev - 'ry way.

4
ev - 'ry way.

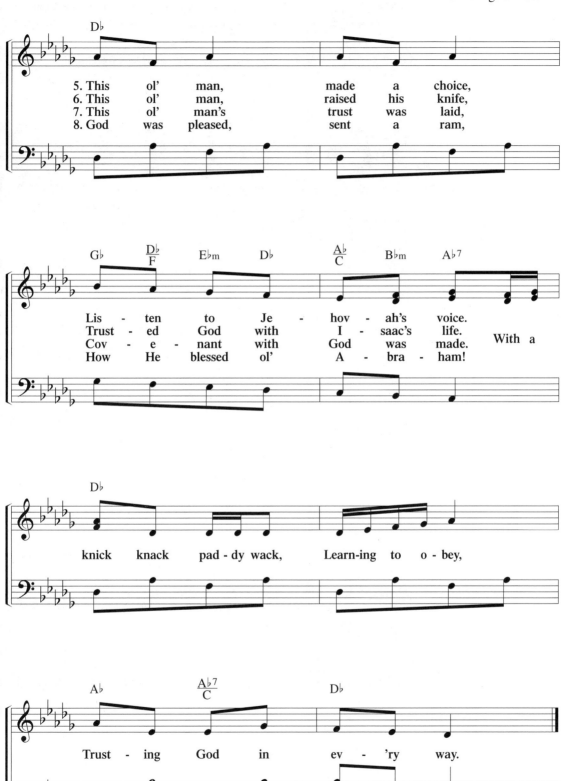

5. This ol' man,   made   a   choice,
6. This ol' man,   raised   his   knife,
7. This ol' man's   trust   was   laid,
8. God was   pleased,   sent   a   ram,

Lis - ten   to   Je - hov - ah's   voice.
Trust - ed   God   with   I - saac's   life.   With a
Cov - e - nant   with   God   was   made.
How   He   blessed   ol'   A - bra - ham!

knick   knack   pad - dy wack,   Learn-ing   to   o - bey,

Trust - ing   God   in   ev - 'ry   way.

56

Fishers of Men

Words and Music by
HARRY D. CLARKE

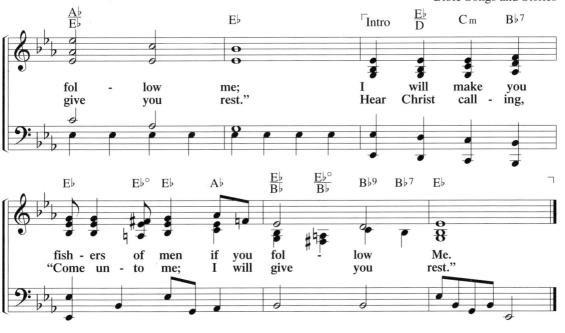

fol - low me; I will make you
give - you rest." Hear Christ call - ing,

fish - ers of men if you fol - low Me.
"Come un - to me; I will give you rest."

I John 4:8 57

Adapted from Scripture

Traditional
Arranged by David McDonald

♩ = ca. 126

The Bi - ble tells us God is love,

God is love, God is love. The Bi - ble tells us

God is love. Let's share God's love.

58 Get in the Ark!

Words and Music by
SUUZANNE H. CLASON

Rat - a - tat - tat and a thump, thump, thump!

No - ah built a great big ark.

Rat - a - tat - tat and a thump, thump, thump! For his

fam - 'ly to em - bark.

Get in the ark; it's go - ing to rain.

*Here come the cows: "moo, moo, moo."

Intro

Get in the ark; it's go - ing to rain.

Here come the an - i - mals two by two.

*Option: Add other verses of animal sounds, but retain sounds of animals already in the ark. For example:

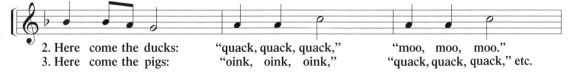

2. Here come the ducks: "quack, quack, quack," "moo, moo, moo."
3. Here come the pigs: "oink, oink, oink," "quack, quack, quack," etc.

59 God Gave Us a Special Book

Words and Music by
RHETT PARRISH, JODI HANNA
and TRISH MENDOZA
Arranged by Ed Kee

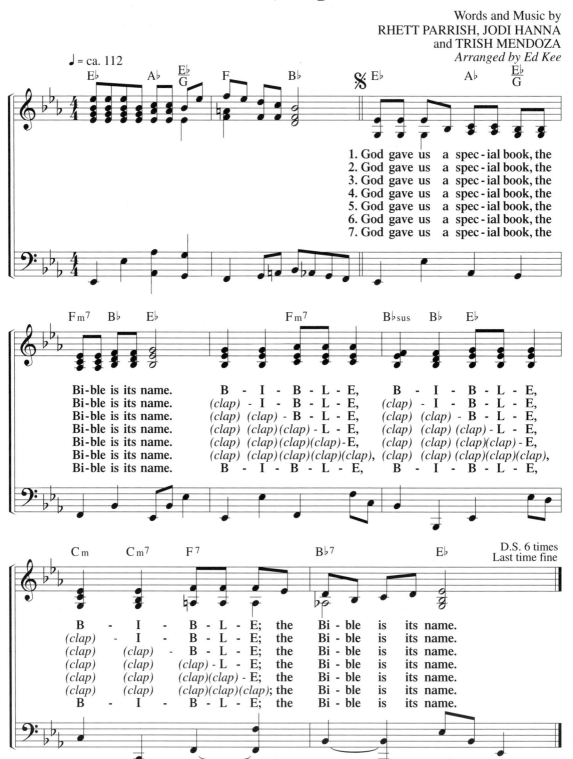

I Am a "C"

Unknown
Arranged by Lyndell Leatherman

*May be repeated several times, with gradually increasing speed.

61 Happy All the Time

Words and Music by
A. B. SIMPSON

1. Point hands inward toward chest.
2. Point hands outward.
3. Point arms up.
4. Point arms down.
5. Cup hands around smiling face.

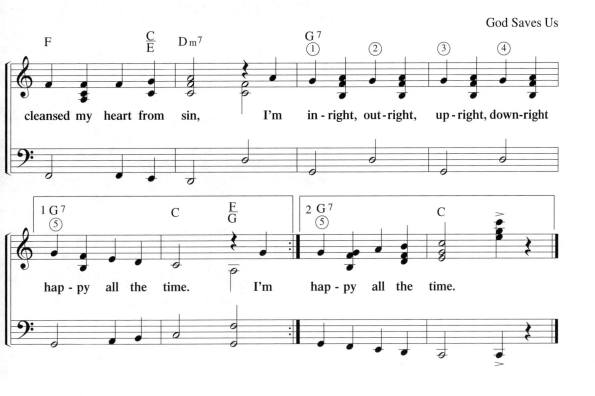

cleansed my heart from sin, I'm in-right, out-right, up-right, down-right

hap-py all the time. I'm hap-py all the time.

Into My Heart

62

Words and Music by
HARRY D. CLARKE

In-to my heart, in-to my heart, Come in-to my heart, Lord Je-sus;

Come in to-day, come in to stay, Come in-to my heart, Lord Je-sus.

63 Joy from Head to Toe

Words and Music by
JANET McMAHAN-WILSON

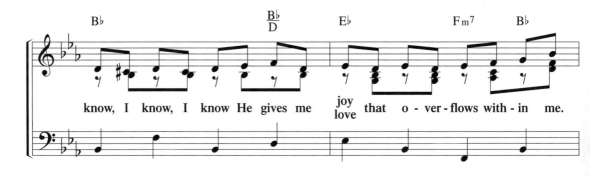

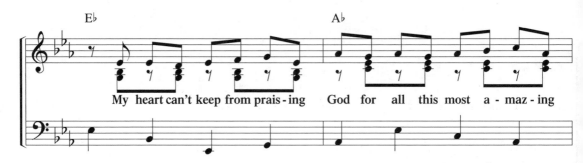

Each time you sing "head to toe," touch your head, then your toes.

God Saves Us

God Saves Us

64

A-B-C-D-E-F-G

Words and Music by
HUBERT MITCHELL

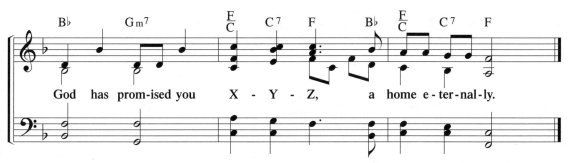

God has prom-ised you X - Y - Z, a home e-ter-nal-ly.

A Special Place 65

Words and Music by
BILL INGRAM

God has made a spe-cial place called Heav-en;____ A place for all who love the Lord to share. It's a place of hap-pi-ness and beau-ty; And best of all— Je-sus will be there.

66 He'll Be Comin' Down from Heaven

DOUG JOHNSON, age 9

Traditional
Arranged by Lyndell Leatherman

A Helper I Will Be

VALERIE A. WILSON

Traditional
Arranged by Kelli Kolesar

1. A helper I will be; A helper I will be. There's work to do; There's work to do. A helper I will be.
2. I'll help pick up the toys; I'll help pick up the toys. There's work to do, There's work to do, I'll help pick up the toys;
3. I'll put a-way the books; I'll put a-way the books. It's sto-ry time; It's sto-ry time. I'll put a-way the books;
4. Let's get our rest time mats; Let's get our rest time mats; It's time to rest, It's time to rest. Let's get our rest time mats;
5. I'll help my mom and dad; I'll help my mom and dad. There's work to do; There's work to do, I'll help my mom and dad.

1. March in place.
2. Pick up toys and put them away.
3. Put away books in the bookcase.
4. Get rest mats and place then on the floor.

OPTIONAL: Sing, "Let's all put on our coats;" "Let's clean up all the paints;" "Let's throw our trash away."

Verses 1, 2 and 5 on recording.

68 Friends Love One Another

Words and Music by
CAROL McCLURE

1. Shake hands with a friend.
2. Join hands in a circle.

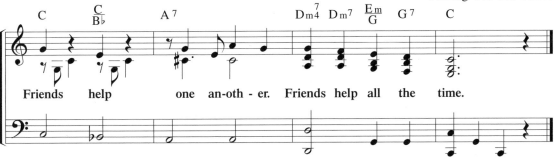

Friends help one an-oth - er. Friends help all the time.

Jesus, I Want to Be Like You 69

Words and Music by
BILL F. LEACH

1. Je - sus, I want to be like You.
2. Je - sus, I want to live like You.
3. Je - sus, I want to love like You.
4. Je - sus, I want to be like You.

Je-sus, I want to be like You. Je-sus, I want to
Je-sus, I want to live like You. Je-sus, I want to
Je-sus, I want to love like You. Je-sus, I want to
Je-sus, I want to be like You. Je-sus, I want to

be like You. I want to be like You.
live like You. I want to live like You.
love like You. I want to love like You.
be like You. I want to be like You.

*Some children may sing the high notes on the vocal tag.

70 Let Us Love One Another

Adapted from I John 4:7

Traditional
Arranged by David McDonald

O Be Careful

Traditional
Arranged by Lyndell Leatherman

1. O be care-ful, lit-tle eyes, what you see; O be
2. O be care-ful, lit-tle ears, what you hear; O be
3. O be care-ful, lit-tle tongue, what you say; O be
4. O be care-ful, lit-tle hands, what you do; O be
5. O be care-ful, lit-tle feet, where you go; O be

care-ful, lit-tle eyes, what you see; For the Fa-ther up a-bove is
care-ful, lit-tle ears, what you hear; For the Fa-ther up a-bove is
care-ful, lit-tle tongue, what you say; For the Fa-ther up a-bove is
care-ful, lit-tle hands, what you do; For the Fa-ther up a-bove is
care-ful, lit-tle feet, where you go; For the Fa-ther up a-bove is

look-ing down in love; So be care-ful, lit-tle eyes, what you see.
look-ing down in love; So be care-ful, lit-tle ears, what you hear.
look-ing down in love; So be care-ful, lit-tle tongue, what you say.
look-ing down in love; So be care-ful, lit-tle hands, what you do.
look-ing down in love; So be care-ful, lit-tle feet, where you go.

Point to the body part mentioned in each verse.

Verses 1, 2, 3 and 5 on recording.

72   This Little Light of Mine

Traditional
Arranged by David McDonald

1. This lit-tle light of mine, I'm gon-na let it shine!

This lit-tle light of mine, I'm gon-na let it shine!

This lit-tle light of mine, I'm gon-na let it shine! Let it

v. 1 — Hold up one finger like a candle.
v. 2 — Cover "candle" with opposite hand and lift off at "NO!"
v. 3 — Blow out the "candle."
v. 4 — Hold up one finger like a candle.

73

My Family

Words and Music by
LEWIS H. and BETTY S. WALKER

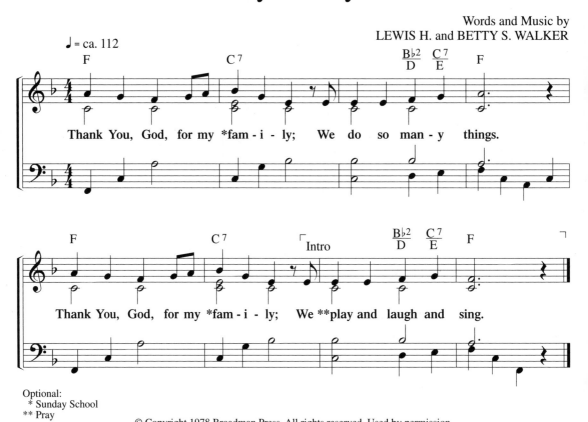

Thank You, God, for my *fam - i - ly; We do so man - y things.

Thank You, God, for my *fam - i - ly; We **play and laugh and sing.

Optional:
* Sunday School
** Pray

74

God Wants Us to Obey

Words and Music by
JANET McMAHAN-WILSON
and TOM McBRYDE

1. God wants us to o - bey each and ev - ery day; In
2. God wants us to be kind, each and ev - ery day; In

Talk about ways we obey God; ways we can show kindness to others.

all we do and all we say, God wants us to o - bey.
all we do and all we say, God wants us to be kind.

I Love My Mommy 75

Words and Music by
JANET McMAHAN-WILSON
and TOM McBRYDE

1. I love my *mom - my and my mom - my loves me, ___ my
2. I love my dad - dy and my dad - dy loves me, ___ my

mom-my loves me, ___ my mom-my loves me. ___ I love my mom-my and my
dad - dy loves me, ___ my dad - dy loves me. ___ I love my dad - dy and my

mom - my loves me. ___ I'm gon - na give her a great big hug.
dad - dy loves me. ___ I'm gon - na give him a great big hug.

*Substitute: teacher ... her/him or a child's name ... her/him

76 The Fruit of the Spirit

Words and Music by
FRANK HERNANDEZ

The fruit of the Spir-it is love, joy, peace, pa-tience, kind-ness, good-ness. The fruit of the Spir-it is faith-ful-ness, gen-tle-ness and self-con-trol. Since we

77

Answer Song

Words and Music by
SUZANNE H. CLASON

Seek Ye First

Words and Music by
KAREN LAFFERTY

79

Now We'll Talk to God

Words and Music by
DOT CACHIARAS

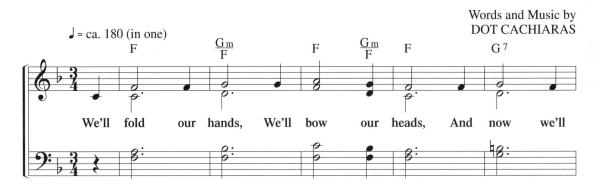

We'll fold our hands, We'll bow our heads, And now we'll

talk to God;___ And now we'll talk to God.___

Motions: Follow the instructions in the text.

80

Sh-h-h-h

Words and Music by
MARIE H. FROST

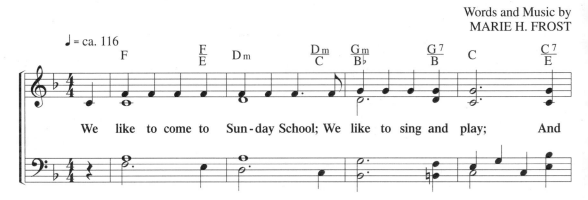

We like to come to Sun-day School; We like to sing and play; And

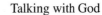

when it's time to talk to God, We fold our hands and pray. *Sh–h–h–h*

(spoken gently)

Anytime, Anywhere

81

Words and Music by
DON PHILLIPS

An-y-time, an-y-where I can talk to God. An-y-time, an-y-where God is there. An-y-time, an-y-where He will hear my prayer; An-y-time, an-y-where God is there.

82 When We Talk to Him

Words and Music by
KEN BIBLE

Church Time

Words and Music by
MARGARET M. SELF

This song works well with melody bells (tone educator bells). Give one note, C through G, to each of five children. Each child plays his note as the teacher points to him or her. Children can pretend to be the clapper in a bell. Have them raise their hands over their heads with palms together. As they sing, "Church time, church time," they should sway back and forth as though part of a bell that is ringing.

84   I Was Glad

Words and Music by
DWIGHT UPHAUS

1. Clap hands as in joy.
2. Cup hands around mouth.
3. Walk in place.
4. Touch fingertips to make house.
5. Point upward.
6. Hold hands to form book.
7. Fold hands.

85   We Go to Church

Traditional

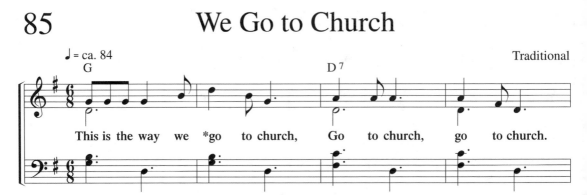

*Substitute: pray in church; sing in church; sit in church; walk in church; etc.

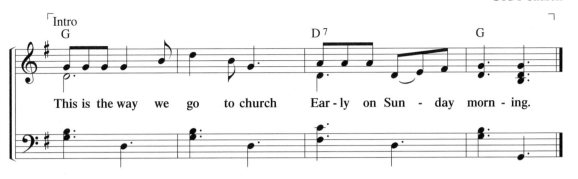

This is the way we go to church Ear-ly on Sun - day morn - ing.

We Are the Church

86

Words and Music by
RICHARD AVERY
and DONALD MARSH

I am the church! You are the church!

We are the church to-geth-er! All who fol-low Je - sus,

All a-round the world! Yes, we're the church to-geth-er.

1. Both hands pointing to self.
2. Both hands pointing to others.
3. Hands open, palms up, arms extended.
4. Point straight up.
5. Arms raised and rotated "around."
6. Shake hands with person nearby.

God's Church

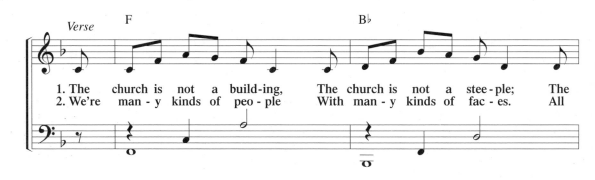

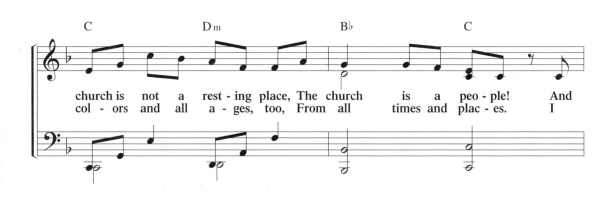

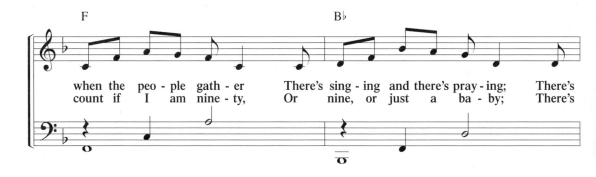

Tell It!

Words and Music by
CINDY BERRY

88
Away in a Manger

Unknown

JAMES R. MURRAY

1. Away in a manger, no crib for a bed, The little Lord Jesus laid down His sweet head. The stars in the sky looked down where He lay, The

2. The cattle are lowing, the Baby awakes, But little Lord Jesus, no crying He makes. I love Thee, Lord Jesus! look down from the sky, And

3. Be near me, Lord Jesus, I ask Thee to stay Close by me forever, and love me, I pray. Bless all the dear children in Thy tender care, And

1. Fold arms as though holding a baby and make rocking motions.
2. Lay head on folded hands.
3. Point upward.
4. Place hand as though shading eyes and look down.

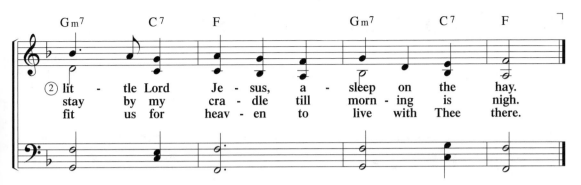

lit - tle Lord Je - sus, a - sleep on the hay.
stay by my cra - dle till morn - ing is nigh.
fit us for heav - en to live with Thee there.

Baby Jesus

89

KATHRYN BLACKBURN PECK   FAITH CHAMBERS WILSON

1. Ba - by Je - sus went to sleep
2. Moth - er Mar - y tucked Him in,

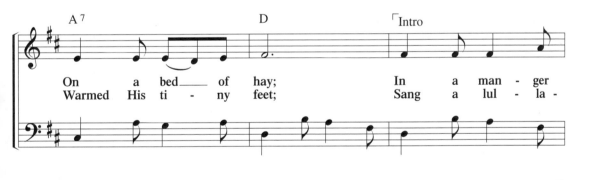

On a bed___ of hay;   In a man - ger
Warmed His ti - ny feet;   Sang a lul - la -

soft and deep   Ba - by Je - sus lay.
by to Him,   "Sleep,___ my Ba - by, sleep."

90 Happy Hallelujah Christmas Song

Words and Music by
JANET MCMAHAN-WILSON
and TOM MCBRYDE

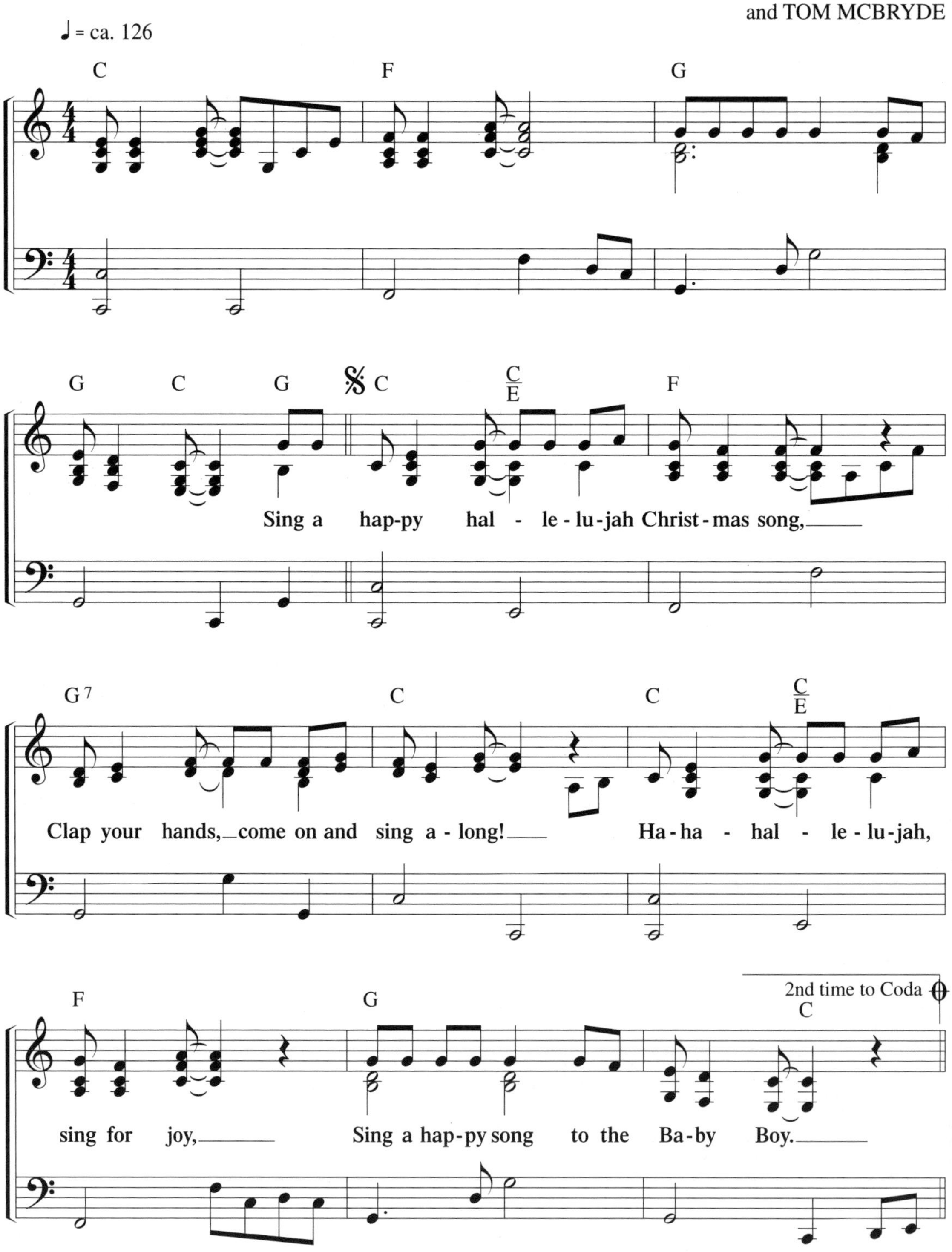

♩ = ca. 126
C F G
G C G C C/E F
Sing a hap-py hal - le-lu-jah Christ-mas song,
G7 C C C/E
Clap your hands, come on and sing a - long! Ha-ha - hal - le-lu-jah,
F G C
2nd time to Coda
sing for joy, Sing a hap-py song to the Ba-by Boy.

Je - sus,_____ Je - sus,_____ Lit - tle, bit - ty Ba - by ly - ing

on the hay;_____ Je - sus,_____ Je - sus,_____

I want to praise You ev - 'ry - day._____ Sing a

Sing a hap - py song to the Ba - by Boy._____

91 Three Wise Men

JANET MCMAHAN-WILSON
and RHETT PARRISH

Traditional
Arranged by Ed Kee

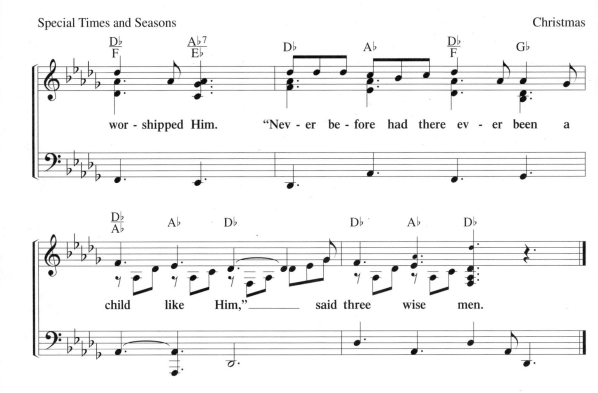

wor - shipped Him.   "Nev - er be - fore had there ev - er been   a

child   like   Him,"_____ said three   wise   men.

92   Christmas Tells of Jesus

Words and Music by
CLAUDE and CAROLYN RHEA

Christ - mas tells of   Je - sus,   born so   long a - go;

Lit - tle   Ba - by   Je - sus,   O   I   love Him   so.

O How He Loves You and Me

93

Words and Music by
KURT KAISER

94

Alive, Alive

Traditional
Arranged by David McDonald

95   Shout Hosanna

Words and Music by
ROBERT C. EVANS

1. Imitate riding donkey
2. Wave hands.
3. Kids crouch and rise up.
4. Point to the sky.

② Wave the branch - es of the trees be - fore Him, Ho -
④ He's a - live, let's tell the world the sto - ry, Ho -

san - na! Ho - san - na! Ho - san - na to the King!
san - na! Ho - san - na! Ho - san - na to the King!

I'm Happy Today   96

VALERIE A. WILSON

MERYL E. WELCH

I'm hap - py, I'm hap - py, I'm hap - py to - day;

For Je - sus is liv - ing this glad Eas - ter Day.

97 Thank You for Freedom

Words and Music by
KEN BIBLE

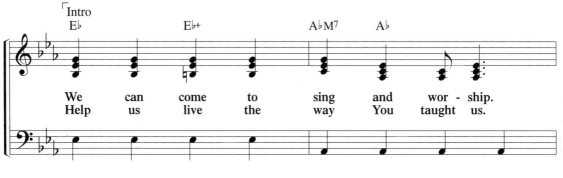

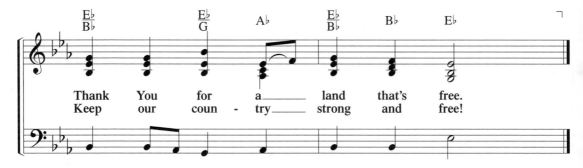

It's Good to Give Thanks

98

Adapted from Scripture

Traditional
Arranged by Lyndell Leatherman

1. It's good to give thanks to the Lord._____ It's good to give thanks to the Lord._____ It's good to give thanks,___ It's good to give thanks,___ It's good to give thanks to the Lord._____

2. It's good to give thanks for our *food._____ good to give thanks for our food._____ It's good to give thanks,___ It's good to give thanks,___ It's good to give thanks for our food._____

3. God cares a-bout **you ev - 'ry day._____ cares a-bout **you ev - 'ry day._____ God cares a-bout you,___ God cares a-bout you,___ God cares a-bout **you ev - 'ry day._____

4. The Lord is my Help - er each day._____ Lord is my Help - er each day._____ The Lord is my Help - er, The Lord is my Help - er, The Lord is my Help - er each day._____

*Substitute names of other things for which children may thank God, such as legs, arms, family members, etc.
**Substitute child's name.

99   O Lord, I Thank You

Traditional
Arranged by David McDonald

life.   I just thank You all the days of my life.

God, We Thank You

100

MARSH QUINN

Traditional Melody
Arranged by David McDonald

1. God, we thank You for this day; Yes, we
2. God, we thank You for our *friends; Yes, we

thank You. God, we thank You for this
thank You. God, we thank You for our

day; Yes, we thank_____ You.
*friends; Yes, we thank_____ You.

Option: Let the children substitute things for which they are thankful, such as food, home, school, church, etc. After the children have learned the song well, divide them into two groups. One group sings pharases 1 and 3, and the other group sings phrases 2 and 4.

101 Jesus, We Just Want to Thank You

GLORIA GAITHER and
WILLIAM J.GAITHER

WILLIAM J. GAITHER

♩ = ca. 108

*1. Je - sus, we just want to thank You.
2. Je - sus, we just want to praise You.
3. Je - sus, we know You are com - ing.

Je - sus, we just want to thank You.
Je - sus, we just want to praise You.
Je - sus, we know You are com - ing.

Je - sus, we just want to thank You.
Je - sus, we just want to praise You.
Je - sus, we know You are com - ing.

Thank You for be - ing so good.
Praise You for be - ing so good.
Take us to live in Your home.

*Recording has verses 1 and 2.

If You're Happy

Traditional
Arranged by Lyndell Leatherman

*Substitute: stamp your feet; say amen; do all three.

103 Say to the Lord, I Love You

Words and Music by
ERNIE RETTINO
and DEBBY KERNER

1. Touch your fin - ger to your nose. Bend from the waist 'way down and touch your
2. Reach your hands up to the sky, Look to the left, then right and blink your

toes; And when you come up slow - ly, start to___ sing, And
eyes; And when you turn a - round you'll start to___ sing,

say to the Lord, "I love___ You. I love___ You, I

love___ You." Say to the Lord, "I love___ You. I

Do as the song tells you to do!

love____You, I love____You." Say to the Lord, "I love____You."

Clapping 104

MARGARET SELF

Adapted from Joseph Hayden

1. Clap-ping, clap-ping, clap-ping, clap, With the hands God
2. Jump-ing, jump-ing, jump-ing, jump, With the feet God
3. Stretch-ing, stretch-ing, stretch-ing, stretch, With the arms God
4. Hop-ping, hop-ping, hop-ping, hop, With the legs God

made for me. Clap-ping, clap-ping, clap-ping, clap,
made for me. Jump-ing, jump-ing, jump-ing, jump,
made for me. Stretch-ing, stretch-ing, stretch-ing, stretch,
made for me. Hop-ping, hop-ping, hop-ping, hop,

With the hands God made for me.
With the feet God made for me.
With the arms God made for me.
With the legs God made for me.

Have children do motions suggested by the words of the song. Let children suggest other actions.

105 I'm So Wonderfully Made

Words and Music by
ROBERT C. EVANS

Optional verse 3: I can stomp my feet. I can jump so high.

106 Hands on Shoulders

Unknown

1. Hands on shoul - ders, hands on knees, Hands be -
2. Hands 'way up high in the air, At your

hind you, if you please. Touch your shoul - ders,
sides, then touch your hair. Hands 'way up high

touch your nose, Touch your hair___ and touch your toes.
as be - fore, Clap your hands,___ one, two, three, four.

Have children do motions suggested by the words of the song.

107 Let's All Sing Together

JOY RAMON

Traditional
Arranged by Joy Ramon

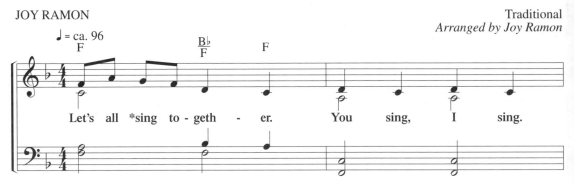

Let's all *sing to - geth - er. You sing, I sing.

*Substitute: clap, tap, jump, march.
"Sing," "jump," "clap," and "march" verses on recording.

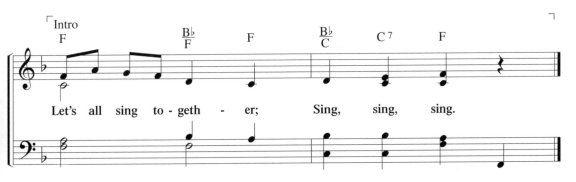

Let's all sing to - geth - er; Sing, sing, sing.

I'm Special
108

Words and Music by
LINDA WATSON

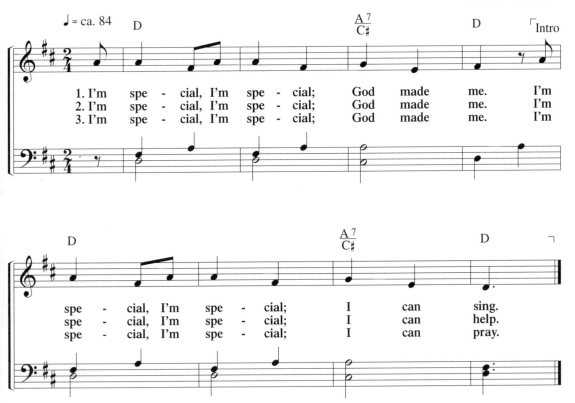

1. I'm spe - cial, I'm spe - cial; God made me. I'm
2. I'm spe - cial, I'm spe - cial; God made me. I'm
3. I'm spe - cial, I'm spe - cial; God made me. I'm

spe - cial, I'm spe - cial; I can sing.
spe - cial, I'm spe - cial; I can help.
spe - cial, I'm spe - cial; I can pray.

109 I Love to Clap My Hands

Words and Music by
JANET McMAHAN-WILSON
and TOM McBRYDE

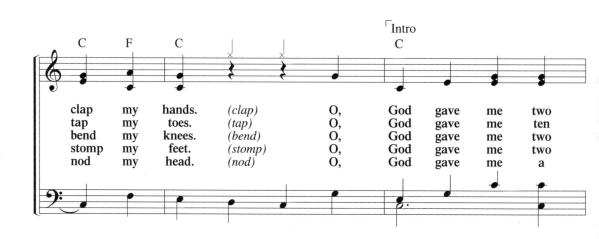

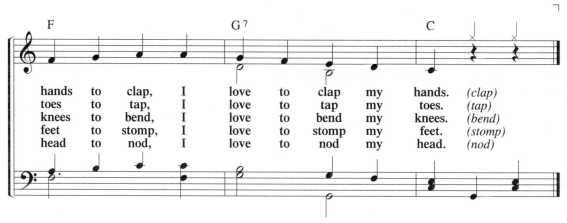

*Recording has verses 1, 2, 3 and 4.

There's No One Exactly like Me   110

TRILBY JORDAN

BETTY ANN RAMSETH

111 Kids Under Construction

GLORIA GAITHER
and GARY S. PAXTON

WILLIAM J. GAITHER
and GARY S. PAXTON

Kids un - der con - struc - tion—

May - be the paint is still wet.

Kids un - der con - struc - tion— The

Fine last time

Lord may not be fin - ished yet.

*1. We're more than just ac - ci - dents with - out the cause; We're
2. Now, mis - ter, I know that I get in your way; I'm
3. Dear Je - sus, please make me more pa - tient and kind, And

more than just bod - ies and brains. God
nois - y and just bug you so. But
help us to be more like You. And

made us on pur - pose; we're part of a plan. He
there's lots of ques - tions I just have to ask If
make room for all oth - er chil - dren of Yours, For

cares and He knows us by name. O!
I'm ev - er go - ing to know. O!
they are still grow - ing up, too. O!

*Recording has verses 1 and 3.

112 Put Together with Love

Words and Music by
MELODY MORRIS

Point to the parts of the body when you sing about them.

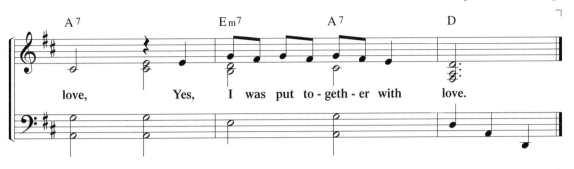

love,   Yes,   I   was   put   to-geth-er   with   love.

The Wiggle Song   113

Traditional

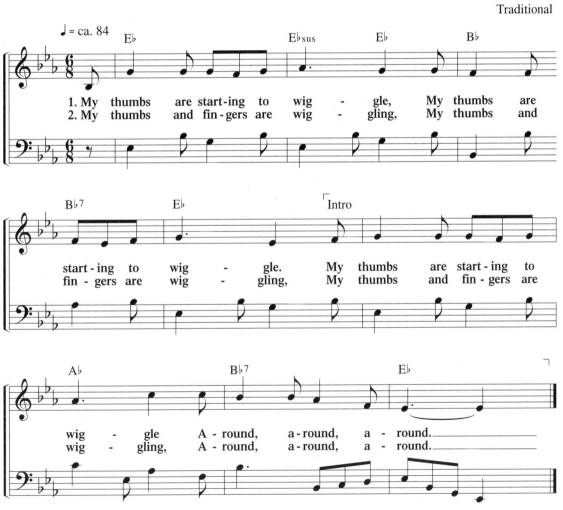

♩ = ca. 84

E♭ · · · E♭sus · E♭ · B♭

1. My   thumbs   are   start-ing   to   wig - gle,   My   thumbs   are
2. My   thumbs   and   fin-gers   are   wig - gling,   My   thumbs   and

B♭7 · E♭ · Intro

start-ing   to   wig - gle.   My   thumbs   are   start-ing   to
fin - gers   are   wig - gling,   My   thumbs   and   fin - gers   are

A♭ · B♭7 · E♭

wig - gle   A - round,   a - round,   a - round.
wig - gling,   A - round,   a - round,   a - round.

Additional verses:
3. My hand is starting to wiggle . . .   5. My head is starting to wiggle . . .
4. My arms are starting to wiggle . . .   6. Now all of me is a-wiggling . . .

114 Colors, Shapes and Numbers

TALMADGE BUTLER

Traditional
Arranged by David McDonald

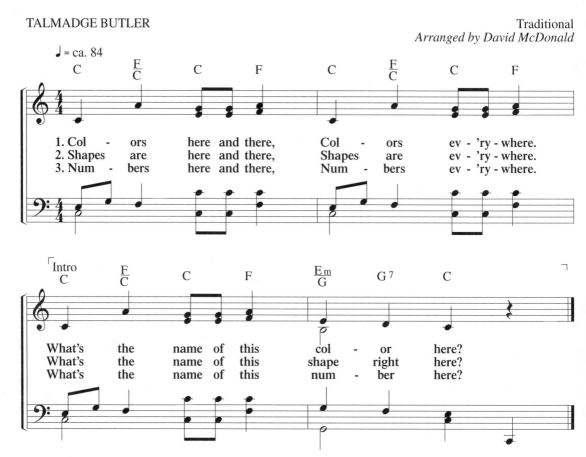

1. Col - ors here and there, Col - ors ev - 'ry - where.
2. Shapes are here and there, Shapes are ev - 'ry - where.
3. Num - bers here and there, Num - bers ev - 'ry - where.

What's the name of this col - or here?
What's the name of this shape right here?
What's the name of this num - ber here?

115 We Are Different!

Words and Music by
VETERIA BILLINGSLEY

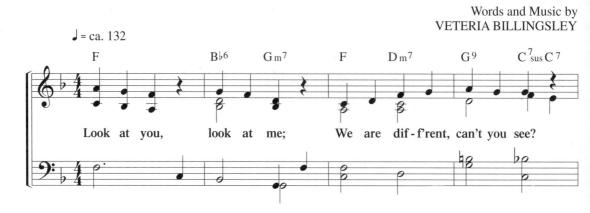

Look at you, look at me; We are dif - f'rent, can't you see?

God made you, God made me; Thank You, thank You, God!

All Fall Down   116

Words and Music by
JANET McMAHAN-WILSON
and TOM McBRYDE

♩ = ca. 80

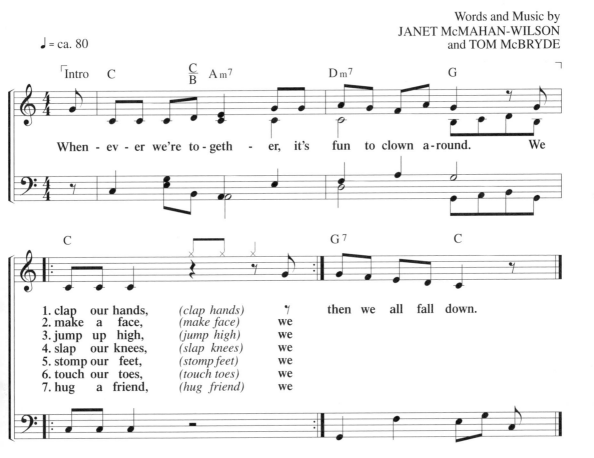

When-ev-er we're to-geth-er, it's fun to clown a-round. We

then we all fall down.

1. clap our hands, (clap hands)
2. make a face, (make face) we
3. jump up high, (jump high) we
4. slap our knees, (slap knees) we
5. stomp our feet, (stomp feet) we
6. touch our toes, (touch toes) we
7. hug a friend, (hug friend) we

Directions for effective useage:
Enjoy this cumulative song with the children, leading them to do the actions suggested. The first time you sing the song, sing and do "clap our hands" only. The second time, add "make a face" to "clap our hands." The third time, add "jump up high" to "make a face" and "clap our hands." Each time you sing the song, add the *new* action first, followed by the other actions already introduced, until finally singing all the way from "hug a friend" to "clap our hands." After "then we all fall down" each time, ask the children to stand up and get ready to sing before beginning again.

117 The Butterfly Song

Words and Music by
BRIAN HOWARD

1. If I were a ① but-ter-fly,_____ I'd thank You, Lord, for
2. If I were an ④ el-e-phant,_____ I'd thank You, Lord, by
3. If I were a ⑦ wig-gly worm,_____ I'd thank You, Lord, that

giv-ing me wings. And if I were a ② rob-in in a tree, I'd
rais-ing my trunk. And if I were a ⑤ kan-ga-roo, You
I_____ could squirm. And if I were a ⑧ bil-ly_____goat, I'd

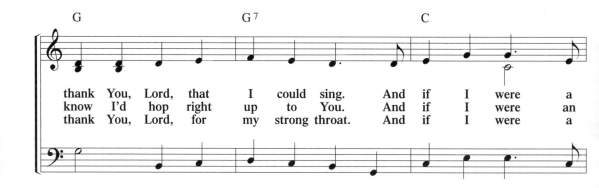

thank You, Lord, that I could sing. And if I were a
know I'd hop right up to You. And if I were an
thank You, Lord, for my strong throat. And if I were a

1. Put hands out to the side to make delicate butterfly wings.
2. Put hands under arms and "flap" like a bird.
3. Swim like a fish.
4. Make a trunk with your arm.
5. Hop like a kangaroo.

6. Wave arms wildly like an octopus.
7. Wiggle.
8. Make "horns" on your head.
9. Make wiggly "ears" on top of your head.

TOPICAL INDEX

ACTIVITY / NOVELTY

A Helper I Will Be 67
All Fall Down 116
Arky, Arky. 43
Clap, Clap, Clap 17
Clapping. 104
Colors, Shapes, and Numbers 114
Get in the Ark! 58
God Gave Us a Special Book 59
God Made Me. 22
Hallelujah! 10
Hands on Shoulders 106
I Am a "C" 60
I Love to Clap My Hands 109
I'm So Wonderfully Made 105
I'm Special 108
If You're Happy 102
Let's All Sing Together. 107
Put Together with Love 112
Say to the Lord, I Love You 103
Shout Hosanna 95
Sing Hallelujah!. 16
Stand Up and Clap 12
The Butterfly Song. 117
The Wiggle Song. 113
This Little Light of Mine 72
Zaccheus 54

BIBLE SONGS

Abraham 55
Arky, Arky. 43
Every Word of the Lord Is True. 44
Fishers of Men 56
Get in the Ark! 58
God Gave Us a Special Book 59
How Did Moses Cross the Red Sea 50
I Open My Bible and Read 45
I Will Listen. 49
I Wonder How It Felt. 40
Jesus Grew and Grew 48
Jesus Loves Me 35
Jesus Loves Me, Me, Me 33
1 John 4:8 57
Love One Another 52
Psalm 119:11 42
The B-I-B-L-E 47
The Wise Man and the Foolish Man 51

There Were Twelve Disciples 41
This Is My Commandment 53
When I Am Afraid 46
Zaccheus 54

CHURCH

Church Time 83
I Was Glad 84
Now We'll Talk to God 79
Sh-h-h-h. 80
We Are the Church 86
We Go to Church 85

CREATION

All Creatures Great and Small 29
Everything Was Made by God 30
God Made Me. 22
God Made the Animals 23
God Saw All. 27
He's Got The Whole World in His Hands . 21
I Love to Clap My Hands 109
I Often Think of God 25
I'm So Glad 24
I'm Special 108
My God Is So Big 14
Praise the Lord, All Creation 19
Put Together with Love 112
That's Good! 26
The Butterfly Song. 117
We Are Different! 115
Who Made You?. 28

CHRISTMAS

Away in a Manger. 88
Baby Jesus. 89
Christmas Tells of Jesus. 92
Happy Hallelujah Christmas Song 90
Tell It! 87
Three Wise Men. 91

EASTER

A-B-C-D-E-F-G 64
Alive, Alive 94
I'm Happy today 96
O How He Loves You and Me 93
Shout Hosanna 95

FAITH
Abraham 55
All Night, All Day. 36
Every Word of the Lord Is True. 44
I Wonder How It Felt 40
My God Is So Big 14
When I Am Afraid 46

GOD'S LOVE & CARE
All Creatures Great and Small 29
All Night, All Day. 36
Clap, Clap, Clap 17
Down in My Heart 13
Enough Love 39
Everything Was Made by God 30
God Cares for You and Me 38
God Is Always There 34
God Is Bigger 37
God Is Love 32
He's Got the Whole World in His Hands . . 21
1 John 4:8 57
I Like to Sing About Jesus 9
I Open My Bible and Read 45
It's Good to Give Thanks 98
Jesus Loves Me 35
Jesus Loves Me, Me, Me 33
Jesus Loves the Little Children 31
Joy from Head to Toe 63
O Be Careful 71
O How He Loves You and Me 93
Praise Him, Praise Him 18
Put Together with Love 112
When I Am Afraid 46
When We Talk to Him 82

HEAVEN & THE SECOND COMING
A Special Place 65
A-B-C-D-E-F-G 64
He'll Be Comin' Down from Heaven 66
I Am a "C" 60
Jesus, We Just Want to Thank You 101

HOLY SPIRIT
The Fruit of the Spirit 76

HOME & FAMILY
A Helper I Will Be 67
I Love My Mommy 75
My Family. 73

INVITATION
A-B-C-D-E-F-G 64
Fishers of Men 56
Into My Heart 62

MISSIONS
Enough Love 39
Jesus Loves the Little Children 31
Tell It! 87

PALM SUNDAY
Ho Ho Hosanna 6
Shout Hosanna 95

PATRIOTIC
Thank You for Freedom. 97

PRAISE & WORSHIP
Alive, Alive 94
Alleluia 4
Clap, Clap, Clap 17
Down in My Heart 13
God Is Love 32
God, We Thank You 100
Hallelujah! 10
He Has Made Me Glad 7
He Is the King of Kings 1
Ho Ho Hosanna 6
I Like to Sing About Jesus 9
I Will Sing Songs of Joy. 11
I'm So Glad 24
It's Good to Give Thanks 98
Jesus Loves Me 35
Jesus, I Love You 2
Jesus, We Just Want to Thank You 101
Let's All Sing Together 107
Make Joyful Noise unto the Lord 5
My God Is So Big 14
O How I Love Jesus 8
O Lord, I Thank You 99
Praise Him, Praise Him 18
Praise the Lord, All Creation 19
Rejoice in the Lord Always 20
Say to the Lord, I Love You 103
Sing Hallelujah! 16
Stand Up and Clap 12
This Is the Day 3
With My Voice 15

PRAYER
Anytime, Anywhere. 81
Into My Heart 62

Now We'll Talk to God 79
Sh-h-h-h. 80
When We Talk to Him 82
With My Voice 15

REJOICING & TESTIMONY

Alleluia 4
Answer Song 77
Clap, Clap, Clap 17
Down in My Heart 13
Happy All the Time 61
He Has Made Me Glad 7
Ho Ho Hosanna 6
I Am a "C" 60
I Like to Sing About Jesus 9
I Was Glad 84
I Will Sing Songs of Joy. 11
Joy from Head to Toe 63
O How I Love Jesus 8
Rejoice in the Lord Always 20
Tell It! 87
This Is the Day 3
This Little Light of Mine 72

SELF-CONCEPT

Clap, Clap, Clap 17
Clapping. 104
God Made Me. 32
I Love to Clap My Hands 109
I'm So Wonderfully Made 105
I'm Special 108
Jesus Grew and Grew 48
Kids Under Construction 111
Put Together with Love 112
The Butterfly Song. 117
There's No One Exactly like Me. 110
We Are Different! 115

SERVING GOD & OTHERS

A Helper I Will Be 67
Abraham 55
Answer Song 77
Fishers of Men 56
Friends Love One Another 68
God Wants Us to Obey 74
I Love My Mommy 75
I Will Listen. 49
Jesus Grew and Grew. 48
Jesus, I Love You 2
Jesus, I Want to Be like You. 69
Let Us Love One Another. 70
Love One Another 52
My Family. 73
O Be Careful 71
Psalm 119:11 42
Seek Ye First. 78
The B-I-B-L-E 47
The Fruit of the Spirit 76
The Wise Man and the Foolish Man 51
There Were Twelve Disciples 41
This Is My Commandment 53
This Little Light of Mine 72
We Are the Church 86

THANKSGIVING

God, We Thank You. 100
He Has Made Me Glad 7
I'm So Glad 24
It's Good to Give Thanks 98
Jesus, We Just Want to Thank You 101
My Family. 73
O Lord, I Thank You 99
Praise Him, Praise Him 18
The Butterfly Song. 117

ALPHABETICAL INDEX

A Helper I Will Be 67
A Special Place 65
A-B-C-D-E-F-G 64
Abraham 55
Alive, Alive 94
All Creatures Great and Small 29
All Fall Down 116
All Night, All Day 36
Alleluia 4
Answer Song 77
Anytime, Anywhere 81
Arky, Arky 43
Away in a Manger 88

Baby Jesus 89

Christmas Tells of Jesus 92
Church Time 83
Clap, Clap, Clap 17
Clapping 104
Colors, Shapes and Numbers 114

Down In My Heart 13

Enough Love 39
Every Word of the Lord Is True 44
Everything Was Made by God 30

Fishers of Men 56
Friends Love One Another 68

Get in the Ark! 58
God Cares for You and Me 38
God Gave Us a Special Book 59
God Is Always There 34
God Is Bigger 37
God Is Love 32
God Made Me 22
God Made the Animals 23
God Saw All 27
God Wants Us to Obey 74
God, We Thank You 100

Hallelujah! 10
Hands on Shoulders 106
Happy All the Time 61
Happy Hallelujah Christmas Song 90

He Has Made Me Glad 7
He Is the King of Kings 1
He'll Be Comin' Down from Heaven 66
He's Got the Whole World in His Hands . . 21
Ho Ho Hosanna 6
How Did Moses Cross the Red Sea? 50

1 John 4:8 57
I Am a "C" 60
I Like to Sing About Jesus 9
I Love My Mommy 75
I Love to Clap My Hands 109
I Often Think of God 25
I Open My Bible and Read 45
I Was Glad 84
I Will Listen 49
I Will Sing Songs of Joy 11
I Wonder How It Felt 40
I'm Happy Today 96
I'm So Glad 24
I'm So Wonderfully Made 105
I'm Special 108
If You're Happy 102
Into My Heart 62
It's Good to Give Thanks 98

Jesus Grew and Grew 48
Jesus Loves Me 35
Jesus Loves Me, Me, Me 33
Jesus Loves the Little Children 31
Jesus, I Love You 2
Jesus, I Want to Be like You 69
Jesus, We Just Want to Thank You 101
Joy from Head to Toe 63

Kids Under Construction 111

Let Us Love One Another 70
Let's All Sing Together 107
Love One Another 52

Make a Joyful Noise unto the Lord 5
My Family 73
My God Is So Big 14

Now We'll Talk to God 79

O Be Careful 71

O How He Loves You and Me 93

O How I Love Jesus 8

O Lord, I Thank You 99

Praise Him, Praise Him 18

Praise the Lord, All Creation 19

Psalm 119:11 42

Put Together with Love 112

Rejoice in the Lord Always 20

Say to the Lord, I Love You 103

Seek Ye First. 78

Sh-h-h-h. 80

Shout Hosanna 95

Sing Hallelujah! 16

Stand Up and Clap 12

Tell It! 87

Thank You for Freedom. 97

That's Good! 26

The B-I-B-L-E 47

The Butterfly Song. 117

The Fruit of the Spirit 76

The Wiggle Song. 113

The Wise Man and the Foolish Man 51

There Were Twelve Disciples 41

There's No One Exactly like Me. 110

This Is My Commandment 53

This Is the Day 3

This Little Light of Mine 72

Three Wise Men. 91

We Are Different! 115

We Are the Church 86

We Go to Church 85

When I Am Afraid 46

When We Talk to Him 82

Who Made You?. 28

With My Voice 15

Zaccheus 54